Home Brew

HOME BREW

By Ben Turner

Based on the Thames Television series

ARGUS
BOOKS
LIMITED

In association with Thames Television

ISBN 0 85242 486 8

First published 1976

Printed in England
by the Garden City Press Ltd
for the publishers
Argus Books Ltd,
14 St. James Road,
Watford, Herts.

Contents

Introduction

This book has been written as an easy-to-follow guide to wine-and-beer-making at home, to accompany the Thames Television series of the same title, *Home Brew,* first transmitted in the summer of 1976. Even if you do not follow the TV programmes, however, you will find this book a useful and comprehensive guide to the subject with all the really essential information presented in logical order, and with illustrations of all the main processes.

1: How it all Began

What Started It?

For at least 10,000 years mankind has been brewing alcoholic beverages of one kind or another, whether it be wine, beer, cider or mead. The ingredients have varied from place to place and generation to generation. In Britain, both ale and mead were popular some 2000 years ago when the Romans came. They brought with them both the vine and the hop but neither were greatly used. Our climate never really suited the vine although apples have always flourished here. The bitter flavour of the hop was not as well liked in ale as the milder flavours of the nettle, yarrow, rosemary, sorrel and similar herbs. Indeed, the hop did not finally supplant other herbs until some 500 years ago.

Women have been the traditional makers of ale, hence the word ale-wife. They also supervised in the still room, where fruit, flower and vegetable wines, meads and ciders were made and stored. Men were more adventurous and developed spirits of different kinds.

Well Done, Henry

Wine made from the fermented juice of fresh grapes was imported by the Roman officers, later by rich merchants and later still by the Abbots and Bishops of the early Church. After the Norman Conquest wines were imported by the Court.

When Henry II married Eleanor of Aquitaine in 1158 the rich wine-lands around Bordeaux became part of England and wine was shipped across the Channel and sold quite cheaply. It was of relatively poor quality, young, rough and cloudy, sometimes even a little vinegary. Cider was much better and growing in popularity.

The Cottage Craft

Honey was used for sweetening and in the 16th and 17th centuries fruit and flower wines were made and sweetened with honey. When sugar was imported cheaply from the West Indies it replaced honey and gave a great impetus to the making of wine at home. Many books of recipes were published but with no knowledge of how fermentation was caused, they mostly produced over-sweet, low alcohol beverages, albeit they were often strongly laced with brandy.

This situation continued until the turn of the present century. Industralisation, the Boer War, the Great War and its economic after-math, virtually killed off these ancient cottage crafts. But not quite. Immediately after the Second World War interest was revived, and more leisure time, better housing, more adult education, holidays abroad, improved social and domestic economy all contributed to the upsurge in the making of wine and the brewing of beer in the home.

Modern Winemaking and Brewing at Home

Winemaking Clubs were started, flourished and multiplied. New books appeared explaining in simple terms the technology of winemaking and brewing. Firms started to market concentrated grape juice and to provide the essential (and non-essential) equipment and ingredients such as acid, tannin, nutrients and yeast. Shows and competitions were organised. A National Association of Amateur Winemakers was formed and in 1963 The Amateur Winemakers' National Guild of Judges. Systems of adjudication were unified and standardised. Candidates were trained and examined in their knowledge of winemaking, the theory of adjudication and a practical test. The passmark was high and membership of the Guild was highly sought and seldom granted or so it seemed. Nevertheless, membership grew from 40 in 1963 to 200 in 1976.

Different Kinds of Winemakers

Three philosophies of winemaking have now developed. There are the 'kits only' group who make a varied selection of wines from cans of concentrated grape juice. They supply their day to day needs for wine at a cost of around 20p per bottle—a regular saving of about 80p on a bottle of imported vin ordinaire. Next come the country winemakers who enjoy their parsnip, elder-flower or blackberry wine as such. They enjoy the simple direct flavours and have no desire for complicated recipes, the use of an hydrometer and so on. The third group are the true amateur winemakers who blend together different ingredients to produce a wine similar in quality to the well known wines of France, Germany and Italy, Spain and Portugal. Often for less than 15p a bottle they can produce wines equivalent in quality to those costing up to £3 a bottle. The great saving, of course, is in Excise Duty, labour costs, overheads, transport and the like. Bottles, too, are used over and over again.

Drink it Yourself

Whilst wine may be freely and cheaply made at home for domestic consumption it is illegal to make wine for sale unless one has first obtained a licence to do so and paid the appropriate taxes. It is also illegal to distil wine of any kind in any way and readers are strongly recommended not to try. Be content with making excellent wine and drinking it at home with family and friends.

2: Making Wine and Beer the Easy Way

Wines You Can Make

Thousands of winemakers regularly make wine from cans of concentrated grape juice blended to produce wines similar in type to the wide variety of commercial wines now available from supermarkets and wine shops. The range extends from Vermouths and dry sherries through white, red and rosé table wines to dessert wines like cream sherry, port and madeira. Moreover a wide choice of manufacturers enable the winemaker to select by trial and error the concentrate that produces the kind of wine that he or she prefers.

What Does It Cost?

Most concentrates require the addition of some sugar as well as water and, of course, yeast, but at least one range is manufactured that requires no sugar. At the time of going to press the average cost was around 20p per bottle of wine produced. Some cost a little less, some a little more. The quality was fairly uniform, although some manufacturers produced certain blends better than others. But much of this is a matter of opinion.

Where to Buy Them

The widest range of concentrates is stocked by Messrs Loftus of Charlotte Street, London W1, but the larger branches of Boots the Chemist stock a wide selection and so do nearly all of the Home Brew shops that can be found in almost every town. Some gardening centres also stock grape concentrates as well as some supermarkets and shops like Woolworths.

Opposite: A selection of the equipment and ingredients used in winemaking at home. Everything is available from shops specialising in home winemaking supplies.

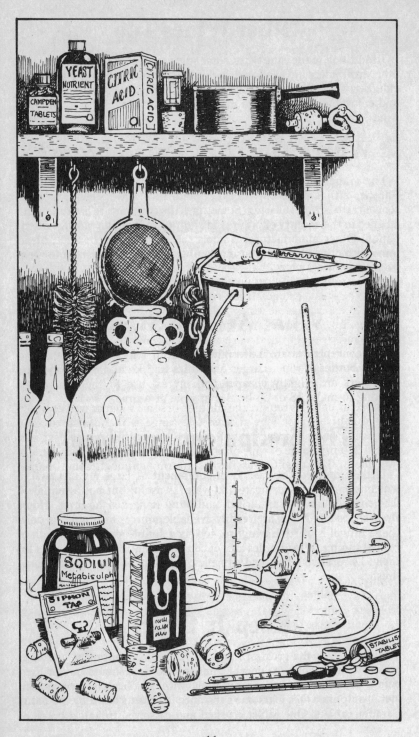

11

Other Wines Too

In addition to the wine types, some splendid blends of grape juice and other fruit juices are available, including apricot, bilberry, blackberry, elderberry, gooseberry, morello cherry etc. These make very interesting and enjoyable wines, though naturally different from the commercial wines.

Where Do They Come From?

The grapes used are mainly grown in Spain, Cyprus and Eastern Europe, although recently France and Italy have been exporting concentrated grape juice too. Sometimes the concentrate is canned and labelled in the country of origin and shipped to Britain ready for distribution. Other manufacturers import the concentrates in bulk, blend some with others, add flavourings and can, label and distribute them from their own factory.

What Are the Sizes?

The concentrates are uniformly packed in 1 kg cans, sufficient to make 6 bottles of wine. Larger quantities in 3 kg and 6 kg polythene containers are slightly cheaper and of real use to the winemaker wanting to make 18 or 36 bottles of wine at a time.

The Equipment You Need

Little is required in the way of equipment. A large jug or vessel in which to mix the concentrate and water is useful but not essential. A fermentation jar and an airlock and bung is needed however. Home Brew shops and Boots are readily available sources of supply. A polythene funnel is worth having; so, too, is a simple siphon or length of rubber tubing. Wine bottles are, of course, essential and new corks for them. Decorative labels and capsules give your bottles a professional finish.

Keep It Clean

Hygiene is of the greatest importance and all equipment and containers with which the wine will come into contact should be sterilised before use. This is very simply done with a solution of potassium metabisulphite. This fearsome substance is better known by the name Camden tablets. One tablet crushed and dissolved in half a bottle of cold or tepid water is sufficient. Swirl the solution around the jar and pour it through the funnel into bottles. It may be poured from bottle to bottle and safely sterilises all the surfaces it touches. Its effectiveness is increased by the addition of a few citric acid crystals.

Start Making Now

First then, select a can of concentrate of your choice. Detailed instructions come with each can and vary slightly from one manufacturer to another. In general, however, all you have to do is open the can or container and pour the contents into a fermentation jar. Rinse out the container with tepid water so as not to waste any concentrate. Add this to the jar and then pour in another 3 or 4 containers-full until the jar is about five-sixths full. Give the contents a good swirl or stir, then add the contents of a sachet of yeast, preferably of the same kind as the concentrates, eg, a sauternes yeast with a sauternes concentrate.

Don't Forget the Airlock

Soften the bored bung in warm water and then carefully push the tube of the airlock into the hole of the bung—as far as it will go to ensure

Two types of airlock (or fermentation lock) showing method of inserting it through the bung. Bottom right shows the method of fermenting a sherry "must".

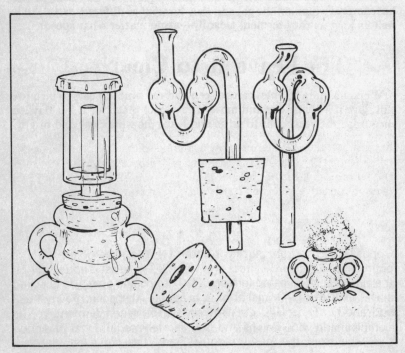

a good tight fit. Pour a little water in it to form the lock and then tightly press the bung into the neck of the jar. Fix a label describing the contents and date, then stand it in a nice warm place near the kitchen boiler, or a radiator, the airing cupboard or wherever is consistently warm—around 20° to 24°C (68-75°F).

Fermenting Already

Within a day or two bubbles will be seen in the contents of the jar and lozenges of escaping gas, called carbon dioxide, will be seen passing through the water in the air lock. The purpose of this little gadget is to prevent air, dust and spoilage organisms, from getting into the wine, whilst permitting the gas formed during fermentation to escape.

Add Some Sugar

After 7 or 8 days some wine must be withdrawn from the jar so that some sugar, usually about 140 grams (5 oz) may be dissolved into it. Pour this back slowly to prevent frothing. Refit the airlock and return the jar to its place. About a week later—the time is not critical—repeat the process, top the jar up to the neck with cold water and leave the wine to finish fermenting, usually about another week to 10 days.

Some wines ferment more quickly than others so do not worry if you have several wines 'on the go' and they ferment at different rates. All is well as long as they ferment steadily—at no matter what speed.

Leave It to Clear

When no more bubbles can be seen and the wine appears to be quite still, give it a gentle stir and move it to a cool place for a few days to encourage the yeast cells to settle and leave the wine clear and bright.

Opposite, left to right, top to bottom (1) The juice concentrate is poured into 6 pints (3½ litres) of water. (2) The yeast is added. (3) Fit the airlock and leave it to ferment. (4) The specific gravity is checked and at 1.010 5 oz (140 gms) of sugar is added. At specific gravity 1.002 add another 5 oz (140 gms) of sugar. (5) When fermentation is complete add wine finings and Camden tablets. (6) Filter or siphon the wine from the jar into bottles, add the corks and labels.

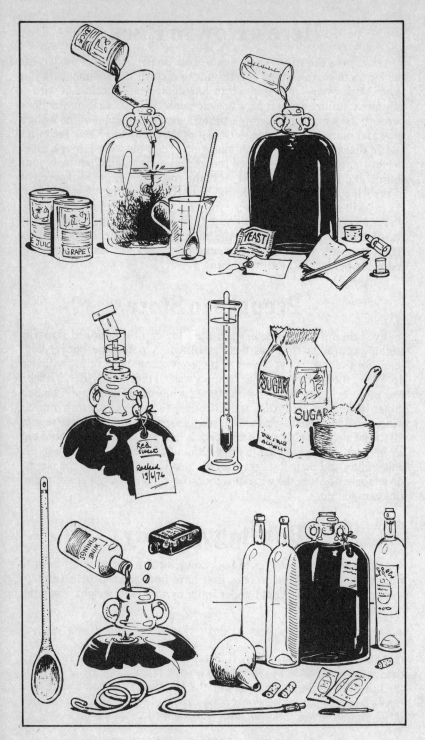

Here's How to Rack

As soon as a line of sediment can be seen on the bottom of the jar, lift the jar on to a table being careful not to disturb the sediment. If you have another jar—and it is worth having several—sterilise it with a sulphite solution, drain it for a few moments, then place it on the floor beneath the jar of wine. Remove the airlock, take one end of the siphon tube and place it in the wine well clear of the sediment. Place the other end of the tube in your mouth and gently suck the wine into the tube. When the tube is full squeeze the end in your mouth between your thumb and forefinger and place it in the empty jar. Because the weight of the wine in the tube outside the wine is greater than that inside it, gravity will steadily pull the wine from the jar above to the jar beneath. As the level of the wine falls in the jar above, carefully tilt it so that the end of the tube remains in the wine but always clear of the sediment. In this way nearly all the clear wine can be transferred leaving only the sediment behind to be thrown away.

Prepare to Store

If you do not have a second jar, the wine can be siphoned into any suitable container that has been sterilised. A polythene bucket kept solely for the purpose of winemaking, a very large bowl or jug will also do. When the fermentation jar is empty wash it thoroughly, drain it for a few minutes, then refill it with the clearing wine. Add one Camden tablet to prevent oxidation and infection, top the jar up with similar wine, or cold boiled water, or sterilised glass marbles. The objective is to fill the jar so that only a small air space is left. Whilst a small amount of air helps to mature a wine, a large amount causes the wine to lose life and vitality and taste flat and dull. Fit a softened bung into the jar, tie on a label and store the wine in a cool place: the larder, a spare room, the garage, etc.

Bottling Already

After a couple of months in bulk store, siphon the wine into sterile wine bottles, fit softened corks that have been soaked in a sulphite solution overnight and held under water by a suitable weight. Keep the

Opposite: Here's how to siphon. Place the full jar on the higher level, the empty jar at least its own depth below it. Suck the wine through the tube. When the tube is full, grip the end hard between thumb and forefinger and place the end of the tube in the jar. (With a greater difference in levels the wine will flow faster.)

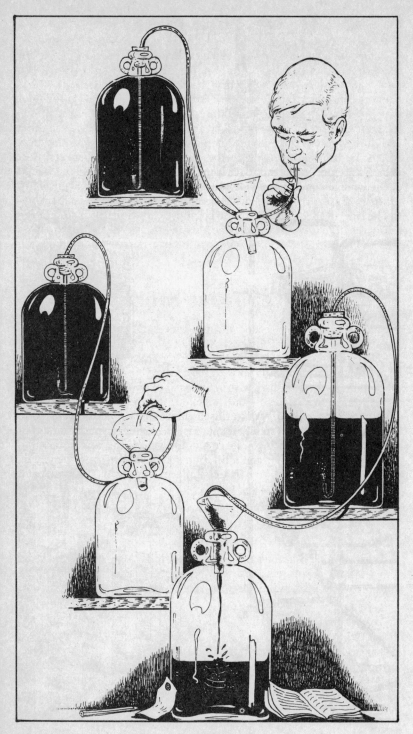

wine for a few more weeks before serving. The wine may, of course, be drunk as soon as it tastes good to you. Experience shows that the wine continues to improve if kept for a year.

But Don't Drink It Too Soon

The sensible winemaker, knowing the temptations, makes wine at regular intervals so that there is always some more coming along. At the bottling stage some half size bottles are used—say 4 full size and 4 half size—the latter are tried first, thus giving the full size bottles longer to mature.

Bottle cartons obtainable free from most supermarkets make suitable storage racks. They can be placed on their side and built up to form any shape to fill the space available—under the stairs for example or better still, under the floorboards—a real cellar this.

Opposite: Methods of racking and storing. On the left mature wine is bottled and in racks. On the right jars are stored for maturing.

3: Better Beer for Everybody

What It's Made From

Beer is made by fermenting a solution of malt, flavoured with hops. It is a great thirst quencher and can be consumed within a few weeks of brewing. It is the traditional drink for Anglo-Saxons. A thousand years ago the young men vied with each other to drink the full of a long cattle horn. Today they can show off drinking 'a yard of ale' in one go.

Over the years it was noticed that some water brewed better beer than others. Burton-on-Trent became famous for its bitter beers because of the gypsum in its spring water. Conversely London became well known for its brown ales and stouts because of its somewhat softer water.

All the different styles of beer can be made in the home from factory prepared kits containing the right malt extract and hop essence or from malt extract and hops or from malted grains and hops.

What Kind of Beer?

As with grape juice concentrate, a good number of manufacturers offer a wide selection of prepared kits that need only some sugar, water and yeast to make from 16 to 40 pints of the beer style of your choice, whether it be lager, pale ale, brown ale, stout, barley wine, etc.

What Do I need?

You need a polythene bin or large bucket in which to prepare and ferment the beer, a siphon and sufficient proper beer bottles with screw stoppers or crown caps in which to store the beer while it matures. Alternatively, a pressure keg may be obtained so that you can draw off a glass of draught beer at the turn of a tap.

The Easy Way

Select the beer style of your choice, open the can and pour the contents into some warm water already in the bin. Wash out the can

Opposite: Home brewing materials and equipment, including a pressure cask to hold beer on 'tap', and the necessary bottles, receptacles and ingredients. Some typical beer kits are also shown.

with hot water to dissolve the last traces of malt and add this to the bin. Add the sugar. Stir well till all is dissolved, then top up with cold water to the required quantity. Add the yeast, cover the bin and leave in a warm place 21° C (70°F). On the third day skim off the dirty froth and wipe the yeast line from around the bin. Re-cover, leave for 2 more days then repeat the process.

Fermentation will finish after 7 to 8 days and the beer will begin to clear. Finings may now be added but are not essential since the beer will, albeit more slowly, clear of its own accord. Move it to a cool place for a couple of days, then carefully siphon it into sterilised beer bottles as already explained in the last chapter.

Don't Forget the Priming

Add a level 5ml spoonful of sugar to each pint bottle, then tightly screw on the stopper or crimp on the crown cap. Shake the bottle to dissolve the sugar and test the seal, then leave the bottle in a warm room for one week while the beer is conditioned by the secondary fermentation in the bottle. Move the bottles to a cool store and keep for a week or two longer, while the beer matures. It will keep for many months, improving steadily, but may be drunk as early as you like it. Each can will have full instructions on the label and vary slightly. In general they are as simple as just described.

Better Beer

Malt extract and hops give more flexibility in making a beer to suit your particular palate. You can, for example, increase the quantity of malt to the sugar or the quantity of hops. You may add some black malt grains, oatmeal or lactose to make different stouts. You may add hardening salts to make bitter if you live in a soft water area. You may add adjuncts such as flaked maize or rice or barley to improve the body, texture and flavour. You may use different kinds of hops such as Fuggles or Goldings or Hallertau to obtain different flavours. In fact you can regularly and easily make a beer that is quite individual to you. The various beer recipes are set out on the following pages.

BASIC BEER RECIPE

1 kg malt extract	(2¼lb)
500 g sugar	(18 oz)
50 g hops	(2 oz)
9 litres water	(2 gallons)

Beer yeast

Dissolve the malt extract and sugar in some warm water, add the hops and boil all together for 45 minutes. Strain the liquor into a sterilised bin containing some cold water. Wash the hops in some hot water to remove the last traces of malt essence and strain this into the bin. Top up with cold water, add the yeast, cover and ferment as already described. This makes 16 pints after racking.

Some variations worth trying:

BROWN ALE

1 kg malt extract	(2¼lb)
250 g crushed chocolate malt grains	(9 oz)
100 g lactose	(3½ oz)
100 g flaked rice	(3½ oz)
100 g brown sugar	(3½ oz)
50 g Fuggles hops	(2 oz)
9 litres water	(2 gallons)

Beer yeast

Dissolve the malt extract in warm water. Add the grains, rice and hops and boil steadily for one hour. Strain into a bin, wash the hops and grains with hot water and add this to the bin. Stir in the sugar and lactose, then top up with water. Add the yeast, cover and ferment as already described.

DRY STOUT

1 kg malt extract	(2¼lb)
250 g crushed black malt	(9 oz)
500 g white sugar	(18 oz)
75 g Fuggle hops	(3 oz)
9 litres water	(2 gallons)

Stout yeast

Method as just described.

LIGHT ALE

1.2 kg malt extract	(2½lb)
1.2 kg white sugar	(2½lb)
140 g hops	(5 oz)
Water to 22½ litres	(5 gallons)
Beer yeast	

Method as basic recipe.

BITTER

1 kg malt extract	(2¼lb)
250 g crushed pale malt grains	(9 oz)
100 g flaked maize	(3½ oz)
250 g white sugar	(9 oz)
75 g Golding hops	(3 oz)
9 litres water	(2 gallons)
Beer yeast	

Method as already described.

Opposite, left to right, top to bottom: *Using hopped malt extract* (1) Pour extract into warm water. (2) Add sugar and stir thoroughly. *Using a dry ingredients kit* (3) Boil the hops and grain. (4) Pour the resulting liquor over the sugar and malt flour. *Both methods* (5) Top up, check temperature. (6) Add the yeast at 60 F (15 C). (7) Ferment, checking specific gravity. (8) Siphon into bottles and add the primer. (9) Hammer on the crown caps and add labels.

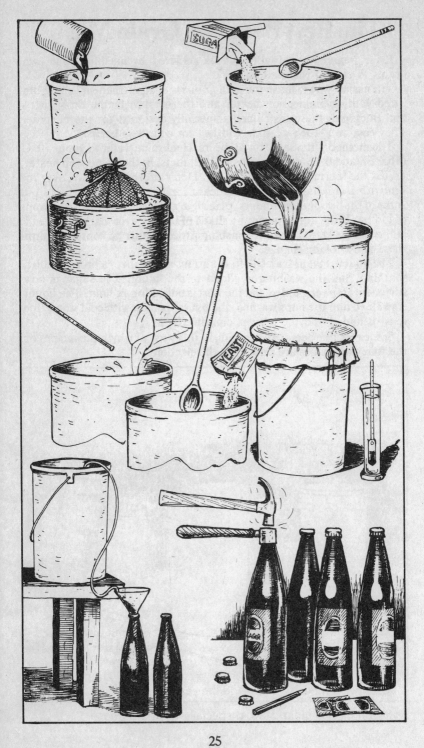

The Best Beer—A Grain Mash

Even greater individuality can be achieved by mashing your own grains to extract the maltose.

The easiest way to mash the malt grains is in a polythene mashing bin fitted with an immersion heater and thermostat. Home Brew shops and Boots sell these instruments specially designed for the purpose. They cost only a few pounds and last for countless brews.

The method is the same for all beers. Heat some water to about 70° C (165°F), add the crushed grains and adjuncts, fit the immersion heater, adjust the thermostat to 152°F (NB. Don't exceed 155°F). Cover the bin with insulating material and leave for from 2-4 hours. Take out some of the liquor after 2 hours, place it in a saucer, and add a few drops of iodine. If the liquor turns any shade of blue or even darkens, then it still contains starch and the mashing process must be continued until there is no colour change.

The liquor is then strained off, the grains are washed, a process called sparging, and the washing is added to the liquor. The sugar is now stirred in. Hops are added and the wort is boiled for an hour. The liquor is strained and the hops washed, the bin topped up with cold water, the yeast is added and the process continued.

Some very fine beers can be made in this way, of which the recipes on the following pages are only a small selection.

Mashing bin for grain, as sold specially for the purpose.

26

INDIA PALE ALE

To make 5 gallons (With acknowledgements to Dr John Harrison)

Mash at 150 F

4 kg crushed pale malt	(9½lb)
250 g crystal malt	(9 oz)
250 g wheat malt	(9 oz)
150 g Goldings hops	(5½ oz)
15 g Northern Brewer hops	(½ oz)
Water to 22½ litres	(5 gallons)
Brewers yeast	

Heat 2½ gals water to 165°F and sprinkle in the crushed malts. Mash at 150°F for 2½ hours or longer if necessary. Strain, wash and discard the grains. Add only five-sixths of the Golding hops and all of the Norther Brewer hops to the wort and boil vigorously for 1 hour. Strain, wash and discard the hops, top up the liquor with cold water and check the specific gravity. If necessary adjust with white sugar to specific gravity 1.050. Cover and leave for three days, then skim off the surface yeast and add the remaining hops, squeezing them in the beer to make sure that they are thoroughly wet. Re-cover and leave for 5 days while fermentation finishes. Strain into a suitable container and leave in a cool place for the yeast to settle. Siphon into sterilised bottles, prime with 1 level teaspoonful castor sugar per pint, stopper or cap and keep for 3 months to mature.

BARLEY WINE

To make 3 gallons (With acknowledgements to Mr Wilf Newsom)

2 kg crushed pale malt	(4½lb)
25 g whole black malt	(1 oz)
15 g gypsum	(½ oz)
500 g crushed crystal malt	(18 oz)
125 g wheat syrup	(4½ oz)
100 g Golding hops	(3½ oz)
Demerara sugar and water to S.G.1.080	

Blend of brewers stout yeast and wine champagne yeast and nutrient.

Heat 2 gals of water to 165° F, add the crushed malts and the whole malt and mash between 145°and 155°F for from 2-4 hours. Strain and sparge. Add the wheat syrup, gypsum and hops and boil for 45 mintues. Strain, wash and discard the hops. Top up with cold water and adjust to specific gravity 1.080 by stirring in approximately 3lb demerara sugar. When the temperature falls to 68°F, pitch an active beer yeast. Cover and leave it in a warm place. After 3 days, skim off the surplus yeast head, stir in the Champagne wine yeast and nutrient, pour the liquor into fermentation jars, fit air locks and ferment in a warm place.

When fermentation has finished, check the specific gravity, which may now be as low as 0.996 and in any case not above 1.004. Rack into sterilised jars and leave to clear. As soon as the barley wine is bright, siphon it into half pint or ¼ litre sterilised beer bottles. Prime each bottle with ½ teaspoonful castor sugar. Then tightly crimp on crown caps. Leave the bottles in a warm room for 2 weeks, then store for 10 months before serving.

LAGER

To make 5 gallons.

4 kg Crushed Lager malt	(9lb)
750 g Brumore malt flour	(1lb 10 oz)
250 g Crushed crystal malt	(9 oz)
125 g Hallertau hops	(4½ oz)
23 l soft water—(or add softening salts)	(5 gallons)
Lager yeast (Saccharomyces carlsbergensis)	

Mash the malts for 2 hours at 142°F and then for two hours at 130°F, until conversion is complete and there is no change of colour in the iodine test. Strain and sparge as usual then vigorously boil the wort with the hops for 45 mintues. Strain, wash the hops, top up with cold water and when the temperature is 60°F check the SG. If necessary adjust to 1.050 or thereabouts. Pitch an active Lager yeast and ferment in the *coolest* place available, around 50°F or lower seems best. Fermentation is naturally slow and may take as long as 3 months. As the beer clears, bottle, prime and store for two months before serving.

The important factors are:
1. Lager malt
2. Lager hops
3. Lager yeast
4. Cold fermentation
5. Long storage

4: Country Wines

Good for You

At one time many country wines were thought to be beneficial to people suffering from certain disorders of the body. Celery wine, for example, was thought to ease the pains of rheumatism, dandelion wine to be good for those with bladder ailments, elderberry wine to be a cure for coughs and colds. The medicine was at least pleasant to take whether it helped or not.

Better Wines

Today, country wines whilst still made in much the same way as in years gone by, are much improved. Better yeasts are used, airlocks are fitted, the role of sugar is more clearly understood, so the wines are stronger and less sweet and, perhaps above all, the benefit of sulphite in sterilising equipment and preventing infection and oxidation is appreciated.

Preparing the yeast as described on the next page. Note the juice required from half an orange, and the sterilised bottle plugged with cotton wool.

What Is It Like?

The fundamental of a country wine is that it is made from a single ingredient and described by that name, eg, celery, dandelion or elderberry. It is usually, though not always on the sweet side and it is often quite strong in alcohol. As a result the wine is often served by itself as what is described as a social wine, ie, a wine to drink during conversation with one's friends, rather than at table with a formal meal, however humble. Country wines often smell and taste of their main ingredient and this is considered by many to be an attribute. It is regarded as an achievement to make a wine that retains the delicious smell and flavour of freshly gathered raspberries or rose petals for that matter. It is by no means an unworthy objective. Here is a basic step-by-step guide to making a typical wine of this type.

MARJORIE GREGORY'S DRIED APRICOT WINE

The wine made in the Thames TV programme by Marjorie Gregory was from dried apricots.

Ingredients:

1lb dried apricots	(450 grams)
2lbs granulated white sugar	(900 grams)

1 lemon and 1 orange—thinly pared rind and juice only
½ saltspoonful grape tannin
1 tsp pectic enzyme

7 pints water	(4 litres)

Hock type wine yeast with a little nutrient plus Vitamin B tablet

PREPARE THE YEAST

Activate the yeast two days beforehand by placing it in a small sterilised bottle with the juice of half an orange, a teaspoonful of sugar, the nutrient and a cupful of cold boiled water. The bottle should be shaken to dissolve the sugar, plugged with cotton wool to keep out dust and germs and placed in a warm situation. Occasionally give the bottle a gently shake to stimulate the yeast.

Then the Apricots

Next day wash the apricots, cut them up, place them in a bowl and cover them with cold water to which 1 Camden tablet has been added to prevent infection and oxidation. The covered bowl should be left overnight.

On the following day the apricots are boiled in the water in which they have been soaking, together with the thinly pared rinds of the orange and lemon. After about 15 mintues the liquor is strained. More water is added to the apricots and peel and they are boiled again for another 15 minutes. When the liquor is finally strained into the pail the apricots may be discarded.

Add the Other Ingredients

2lb sugar is then stirred in and the quantity of liquor should be made up to 1 gallon with cold water. Next the pectic enzyme, tannin, lemon and orange juice, crushed vitamin tablet and active yeast are added. The must is given a good stir, the lid is fitted and the pail set in a warm place. The brew is stirred each day for a week and then poured into a sterilised fermentation jar. An air lock is fitted and fermentation is continued. After 1 month the wine is siphoned from its sediment into a sterilised jar and 1 Camden tablet is added. The air lock is refitted and the jar moved to a cooler place.

The Finished Wine

One month later when the wine is clear and bright, it is siphoned into sterilised bottles, corked, labelled and stored for 4 months before serving.

A sweeter version may be made by adding some sugar syrup after the first siphoning and with the addition of the Camden tablet; ½lb sugar in ¼ pint water is adequate.

Dried apricots have a very strong flavour and it is important not to use more to the gallon than the quantity recommended.

Vegetable Wines

Vegetables have to be boiled to extract their flavour and these wines are made in the same way as just described. It is not necessary to add pectolytic enzyme since vegetables do not contain pectin although most fruits do. It is also sufficient to cook them until they are just tender. If they are overcooked and become mashy the wine often remains hazy. Vegetables have no acid in them either and so two teaspoonfuls of citric or tartaric acid crystals should also be added.

4lb vegetables are needed for each gallon of wine. Scrub them really clean, cut out any imperfect portions, chop them up into dice-sized pieces and away you go.

You may use beetroot, carrot, parsnips, potatoes, swede turnip, mangold wurzle, broad beans, runner beans, pea pods, cos lettuce, spinach and celery.

Elderberry Wine the Same Way

Elderberries may also be boiled to extract their flavour and colour. Every piece of stalk should be picked off since this makes the wine very bitter. The berries should also be rinsed in clean cold water to remove the dust and any tiny insects.

Another way for the Fruits

Other fruits are best picked clean from their stalks, washed, crushed or cut up and fermented on the pulp rather than boiled. Stones from peaches, plums, cherries etc should be removed since they also impart an unpleasant flavour to the wine.

When the fruit is crushed it should be dropped into a bin containing some cold water, one crushed Camden tablet and a teaspoonful of pectolytic enzyme. Cover the bin and leave it in a warm place for 24 hours and don't add the yeast and other ingredients until the following day. The sulphur dioxide given off by the Camden tablet not only stops the growth of moulds and bacteria, but also of yeast itself. Never add yeast with sulphite or Camden tablet, but always at least 24 hours later.

Pulp Fermentation

As soon as fermentation starts the carbon dioxide given off by the yeast lifts some of the fruit out of the water. If it is not pushed down every day, the goodness will not be extracted from it and the drying fruit may attract spoilage organisms floating invisibly in the air. During pulp fermentation then, press the fruit down into the water at least once a day and preferably twice. Keep the bin well covered at other times.

After 4-6 days fermentation on the pulp, strain out and press the fruit in a nylon bag, pour the must into a fermentation jar, if necessary top it up with cold water, fit an air lock and continue fermentation.

How Much Fruit and Sugar?

3-4lb fruit and 2lb sugar makes a dry wine. 2½lb sugar medium dry. 4-5lb fruit and 3lb sugar make a sweet wine.
Very sharp fruit such as blackcurrants will not need any lemon juice.

Elderberries and pears do not require any tannin because they already have plenty.

Wines that may be made in this manner include the following:

Apples. Use a mixture of cooking, eating and crab apples—windfalls will do. Use at least 6-8lb prepared apples and 2lb sugar.

Apricots. 4lb after stones have been removed, and 2½lb sugar.

Blackberries. 6lb cleaned fruit, 2½lb sugar.

Blackcurrants. 3lb cleaned fruit, 3lb sugar, no lemon.

Cherries. 5lb mixed cherries, remove stones and stalks, 2lb sugar.

Damsons. 4lb fruit after stones have been removed. 2½lb sugar.

Elderberries. 3lb prepared fruit, ½lb raisins, 3lb sugar.

Gooseberries. 4lb cooking fruit, 2½lb sugar.

Loganberries. 4lb ripe fruit, 3lb sugar.

Mulberries. 5lb ripe fruit, 3lb sugar.

Pears. 6lb prepared hard fruit, 2lb sugar.

Plums. 5lb fruit after stones have been removed, 3lb sugar.

Raspberries. 2½lb ripe raspberries, ½lb sultanas, 3lb sugar.

Redcurrants. 4lb prepared fruit, 2lb sugar, no lemon.

Rhubarb. 6lb prepared fruit, 3lb sugar and 2 lemons.

Sloes. 3lb fresh fruit, 3lb sugar.

5: Sparkling Wine

What Does It Cost?

Few wines conjure up more happiness than sparkling wine. Unhappily commercial sparkling wines are far too expensive for frequent drinking and they are reserved for weddings, christenings and special anniversaries or occasions. Techniques have now been perfected for turning any light alcohol wine into a sparkling wine at home. The result, which may cost 15p a bottle, is at least as good as the cheapest commercial sparkling wine costing around £1.50 and frequently as good as better qualities costing around £2.50 to £3.00.

What Do I Need?

The only special pieces of equipment required are proper champagne bottles, hollow domed plastic stoppers and wire cages to hold them on to the bottle. Only heavy champagne bottles should be used. NO other bottles are strong enough safely to withstand the pressure of a bottle fermentation. An hydrometer is most useful, so too is a Clinitest. Both are strongly recommended but not absolutely essential. The hydrometer enables you to ensure that the wine does not exceed 12% alcohol. The Clinitest enables you to be sure that the wine contains no residual sugar before it is primed and re-fermented.

How to Do It?

Grapes, gooseberries, apples, pears, white and redcurrants are the most suitable ingredients to use.

A dry wine is prepared from a must with a specific gravity not exceeding 1.080. It is fermented with a champagne wine yeast in the normal way until it is completely dry. The usual process of siphoning the wine from its sediment and maturing it for 4 to 6 months in bulk is followed. Then the new technique begins.

Method 'Champenoise'

Provided the wine is star bright, siphon it from any sediment into a sterilised jar. If it is not star bright, add some wine finings in accordance with the manufacturer's recommendation. Leave the jar in a cool situation and as soon as it is clear, siphon it from its lees into the

34

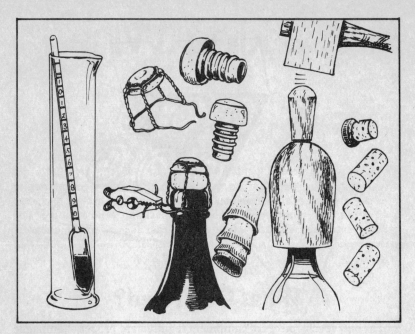

Special equipment for sparkling wines; a hydrometer on the left and plastic stoppers and wire cages in the centre. At right is the contrasting method of corking suitable for still wines.

sterilised jar. Now add 2½ oz caster sugar per gallon and an active champagne yeast, fit an air lock and place the jar in a warm situation, but where you can keep it under observation. As soon as fermentation is thoroughly started, siphon the wine into sterilised champagne bottles and quickly fit sterilised stoppers that have been softened in hot water. Attach the wire cages and secure them firmly. Leave the bottles in a warm room for two weeks while the sugar is fermented, then mature the wine for at least six months and preferably longer. During this time store the bottles on their side.

'Remuage'

A few weeks before the wine is wanted, place the bottle in a box at an angle of 45°, stopper down. Each day for a week give the bottle a little shake and twist of say a quarter revolution so that the sediment comes free from the side of the bottle and slowly slips down towards the hollow stopper. Finally stand the bottle end up in the box giving it the odd twist now and then to encourage all the sediment to slide into the stopper. Leave the bottle in this position for a few days for the sediment to pack down.

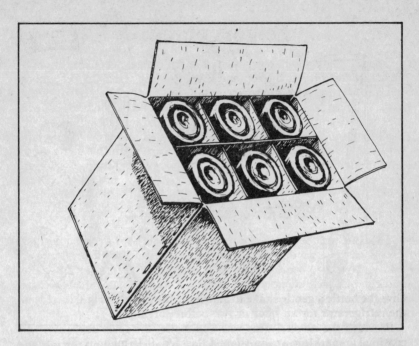

Above: Method of storing known as 'Remuage', as described on the previous page. Box is supported at an angle of about 45°. Below: 'Dégorgement' method as described opposite, with the bottle standing inverted in the ice and salt mixture.

'Dégorgement'

Select a jug or container, such as a child's sand bucket, about 5 inches in diameter at the top and 5 inches deep. Half fill this with a mixture of crushed ice and common salt. Lift up the bottle of sparkling wine, still upside down, and place the stopper and neck of the bottle in the crushed ice and salt. Leave it in this position for 7-10 minutes until the wine in the stopper is completely frozen. Remove the bottle and slowly turn it upright so as not to disturb the carbon dioxide in the wine. Undo the wire cage and then ease out the stopper containing the frozen wine and sediment.

Sweeten to Taste

The wine may be sweetened to suit your taste with a teaspoonful or more of caster sugar dissolved in a tablespoonful of Vodka, or simply by adding from 2 to 4 drops only of a sweetening agent. Do this quite quickly then push home a clean softened stopper and refit the cage. Give the bottle a gentle shake to distribute the sweetness and leave it in the refrigerator for an hour or two before serving.

Provided the original wine was well made, the sparkling wine will continue to sparkle in a tulip-shaped glass for 10-15 minutes after it has been poured. Serve it as an aperitif or on every suitable occasion.

Recurrants make a most attractive pink sparkling wine.

6: The Amateur Wine Maker

As far back as 1835 this phrase was used to describe the countless people then making their own wine in their homes. At that time and for the next 125 years the wines made were exclusively country wines, ie, from a single main ingredient. The emphasis was on making cherry, or gooseberry or elderberry wine as such. It was not until 1960 that the idea of making wines for a specific purpose was first mooted. It has now become the normal method of making wine for many people who might more accurately be described as amateur winemakers rather than country wine makers.

Wine for a Purpose

To achieve an aperitif, a table wine or a dessert wine, the amateur winemaker turns to a variety of ingredients which are blended together to produce a wine comparable in quality to commercial counterparts. Sometimes, indeed, it is not easy to tell the difference.

These winemakers are concerned to get a correct balance of acidity, tannin, alcohol, texture and flavour. They regularly use an hydrometer to measure the amount of sugar in a must or wine. With the information obtained they carefully control the amount of sugar to be added in order to produce a wine of known alcoholic strength.

Acidity

The acidity of various ingredients is studied, tests are made either with pH papers or by titration. Acid in the form of crystals is added whenever it is needed to increase the degree of acidity of a must. Citric, tartaric or malic acid or a blend of all three in the proportions of 2, 2 and 1 respectively, are commonly used. It is recognised that acid is the cornerstone of bouquet and flavour as well as longevity. Without acid a wine tastes medicinal. Dry table wines need 4-5 parts per thousand, sweet dessert wines 6-7 parts per thousand. During maturation the acidity decreases due to chemical interaction in the wine. Often tartaric acid will be precipitated in the form of tiny sandy crystals. The wine becomes mellow as a result. Sometimes malic acid will be converted to lactic acid which has a much milder taste.

Tannin

Tannin too is an essential ingredient of quality wines; it conveys character and distinction. It is usually added in the form of a brown

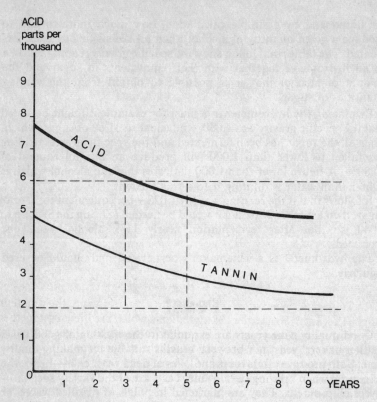

The Acidity chart.
ACID: 7½ ppt reduced to 5 ppt over 7 years.
TANNIN: 3¾ ppt reduced to 3 ppt over 7 years. (ppt = parts per thousand). The best time for drinking this wine is between the 3rd and 5th years.

powder of grape tannin. Some fruits such as black grapes, elderberries and pears already contain sufficient tannin, most fruits and all flowers and vegetables contain no tannin and so it must be added. Usually from one half to a level teaspoonful per gallon—6 bottles—is sufficient. The table above gives a rough guide of the decline in acidity and tannin in a wine during storage.

Hydrometer

The hydrometer is a simple instrument, rather like a thermometer in appearance, used to measure the specific gravity of a liquid. The weight of a liquid, or indeed any substance is always compared with the weight of water at 15°C (59°F). On the hydrometer scale this is taken as 1.000 so a must containing some sugar will weigh more than 1.000. The hydrometer makes it possible to read at a glance the quantity of sugar in the liquid and by a simple calculation, how much more to add to produce a given quantity of alcohol when all the sugar has been fermented. The tables that follow show the specific gravity reading marked on an hydrometer together with their equivalents in sugar and the amount of alcohol that it is possible to obtain from the varying quantities of sugar.

By placing the hydrometer in a must for example it might be noted that the specific gravity was 1.080, equivalent to 31 oz of sugar, which, when all the sugar has been fermented and the specific gravity reading has fallen to lower than 1.000 will produce an alcohol content of 10.89%. A figure lower than 1.000 indicates that the alcohol which is lighter than water is diluting it to a small extent.

It follows that if the reading was say 1.025—i.e. equivalent to 10 oz of sugar, then a further 21 oz sugar would be needed to bring the S.G. up to 1.080, so that after fermentation nearly 11% alcohol would be produced.

The hydrometer is a winemaker's best friend and should be used regularly.

Yeast

Good quality wine yeasts are essential to the making of good wine. Neither bakers' yeast nor brewers' yeast is suitable for making quality wine. Both produce off flavours and piles of dead yeast cells—hence the skimming when brewing beer. Wine yeasts are of the variety saccharomyces ellipsoideus. They are marketed in phials of distilled water, or compressed in a tablet or in granules. Frequently the granules are mixed with some sugar and nutrient crystals so that the yeast cells can be hydrated with a little cold boiled water before use. When the yeast is added to the must, it is then viable and already fermenting. It is always advisable to re-activate a yeast colony before adding it to a must. This ensures that conversion of the sugar in the must will begin as soon as the active yeast is added and minimises the risk of infection due to delay. During activation the yeast cells need plenty of oxygen to encourage them to multiply. When a strong colony is formed, the oxygen supply should be cut off with the aid of an air lock to encourage the yeast to ferment the sugar as rapidly as possible and without further increasing the colony.

Blend the Ingredients

By blending together different ingredients, wine of some character can be formed. A similar result can be obtained by blending together finished wines. Unfortunately not every wine turns out as attractive as one would wish. The fault no doubt lies in the quality of the ingredients used. The situation can be remedied by blending—ie, the mixing of two or more wines together. A short period of maturation is then necessary for the wines to homogenise and improve out of all recognition.

HYDROMETER TABLES

SPECIFIC GRAVITY, SUGAR AND POTENTIAL ALCOHOL TABLES

Specific Gravity	Sugar in 1 gal. lb/oz	4.54 litres kg	Potential Alcohol
1.005	2	.057	0.71
1.010	4	.113	1.39
1.015	6	.170	2.05
1.020	8	.227	2.71
1.025	10	.284	3.42
1.030	12	.340	4.08
1.035	14	.397	4.75
1.040	16	.453	5.44
1.045	1 2	.510	6.13
1.050	1 4	.568	6.79
1.055	1 6	.624	7.47
1.060	1 8	.681	8.18
1.065	1 9½	.724	8.84
1.070	1 11½	.780	9.53
1.075	1 13	.823	10.19
1.080	1 15	.880	10.89
1.085	2 1	.936	11.61
1.090	2 3	.993	12.31
1.095	2 4½	1.036	12.92
1.100	2 6	1.078	13.54
1.105	2 8	1.135	14.24
1.110	2 10	1.192	14.98
1.115	2 11½	1.234	15.62
1.120	2 13	1.277	16.32
1.125	2 15	1.334	17.01
1.130	3 1	1.391	17.70

Note: 2lb sugar dissolved in a liquid occupies 1 pint in volume. 1 kg occupies 62 cls.

Recipes for the most popular different types of wine appear on the following pages.

'CLARET'

A dry red table wine, (Bordeaux style) as demonstrated by Ted Adcock in programme 4 was made from the following ingredients:

1¼lb blackberries, to give a fruity flavour

¼lb dried elderberries (or ½lb fresh) to strengthen the colour and flavour

1 very ripe banana to give body and flavour

½ pint red grape juice concentrate for vinosity and body

2lb sugar for conversion to alcohol

½ oz tartaric acid to bring out the bouquet and flavour

1 tsp yeast nutrient (di-ammonium phosphate)

1 tsp pectolytic enzyme to break down the pectin in the fruit, to extract the flavour and clear the wine

Water to 1 gallon

Bordeaux wine yeast

Camden tablets to provide SO_2 to inhibit infection and oxidation.

Method:

1. Liquidise or mash the blackberries, elderberries and banana, pour on 2 quarts warm water, add the acid, the pectolitic enzyme and 1 Camden tablet, cover and leave for 24 hours.
2. Stir in the grape juice concentrate, the nutrient, an active yeast and ferment for 4 days pressing down the fruit cap twice daily.
3. Strain out the fruit, rolling it round a nylon sieve, stir in the sugar, pour the must into a fermentation jar, top up with cold water, fit an air lock and ferment in a warm place.
4. When fermentation is finished, siphon the clearing wine into a clean storage jar that has been sterilised with a sulphite solution. Add 1 Camden tablet, then cork, label and store the jar in a cool place for 10 months.
5. Siphon into sterilised wine bottles, cork and keep for a further 2 or 3 months before serving free from chill with a meat meal.

Ingredients and some of the stages in making 'claret'.

Ingredients and some of the stages in making 'sauternes'.

'HOCK'

White dry table wine (Hock style) can be made in the same way as just described but from the following ingredients:

    2lb gooseberries—a cooking variety is to be preferred
    (A 2½ size can of gooseberries may be used instead)
    1 very ripe banana—peeled
    ½ pint grape juice concentrate
    2lb sugar
    2 tsp tartaric acid
    1 tsp pectolytic enzyme
    Camden tablets
    Water to 1 gallon
    Hock yeast.

If canned gooseberries are used this wine may be bottled at three months. It is very attractive served cool as a young wine.

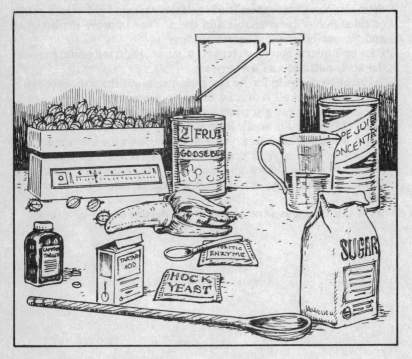

Ingredients for making 'hock'.

'SAUTERNES'

Sweet white wine (Sauternes style):
5lb peaches
5 bananas
2lb sultanas
1 cupful yellow rose petals or elderflowers, lightly shaken
2 tsp tartaric acid
1 tbs glycerine
1lb white firm honey
½lb sugar
1 tsp nutrient
1 tsp pectic enzyme
Camden tablets
Wine finings
Water to 1 gallon
Sauternes yeast.

Method:
1. Peel the ripe bananas. Stone the peaches and wash the sultanas, mash them all up and place them in a bin. If some scented yellow rose petals or elder florets are available add them. They improve the bouquet and flavour but are not essential.
2. Pour on 2 quarts boiling water and when cool add the pectic enzyme, the acid, nutrient and active yeast.
3. Ferment on the pulp for 7 days, then strain out the fruit through a nylon cloth and roll it around but do not press it.
4. Stir in the honey and glycerine, pour it into a fermentation jar, top up with cold water. Fit an air lock and continue fermentation.
5. When fermentation is finished, siphon the new wine into a sterilised jar, stir in the sugar, 2 crushed Camden tablets and some wine finings. Refit the airlock and store in a cool place for 2 weeks.
6. Siphon the clear wine into another storage jar, store for 10 months then bottle.
7. Serve this delicious wine cool with the dessert course of a meal.

'SHERRY'

Aperitif—Sherry type:
2lb large prunes
1lb dried apricots
1lb raisins
2lb sugar
1 oz calcium sulphate—gypsum
½ oz cream of tartar
Pectic enzyme
Nutrient
Water to 1 gallon
Sherry yeast.

Method:
1. Wash and chop up the fruit, place it in a stew pan with 2 quarts of water and simmer it for half an hour. When cool remove the stones, then empty the pulp and liquor into a mashing bin.
2. Stir in the gypsum, cream of tartar, pectic enzyme, nutrient and activated sherry yeast and top up with cold water to 1 gallon. Remove enough liquor to check the specific gravity.
3. Ferment on the pulp for 3 days pressing down the pulp twice daily.
4. Strain out the solids and calculate how much sugar is needed to bring the total SG up to 1.120. For example, if the SG is 1.035 then all the 2lb sugar will be required. If it is lower, then more than 2lb will be needed. Refer to the tables. Stir in half the sugar.
5. Continue the fermentation in a covered bin rather than a fermentation jar since a certain amount of oxidation is necessary to develop the distinctive sherry flavour. After 8 days stir in half the remaining sugar and 8 days later the rest.
6. When fermentation is finished check the specific gravity again. It should be less than 1.000 for a dry wine.
7. Rack the wine into a sterilised jar and if a slightly sweeter wine is required, stir in a small amount of sugar now. Do not fill the jar. Plug the neck with cotton wool.
8. Store in a cool place for 1 year before bottling.

Ingredients and some of the stages in making 'sherry'.

'PORT'

Strong Dessert Wine—(Port style). To make 3 gallons—18 bottles:

2lb bottled bilberries
¼lb rosehip shells (dried)
1½lb elderberries (dried)
2lb apricots (dried)
1 kg grape juice concentrate—red
8lb sugar
2 oz tartaric acid
Nutrient
Pectic enzyme
Camden tablets
Water to 3 gallons
Port yeast

Method:
1. Soak the dried fruit in warm water for 2 hours to enable it to hydrate. Bring it to the boil, simmer it for 20 minutes, then leave it to cool.
2. Pour all this must into a mashing bin and empty into it all the contents of the jar of bilberries. Stir in the acid, the pectic enzyme and two Camden tablets. Cover and leave it for 24 hours.
3. Stir in the grape juice concentrate, half the sugar and a strong colony of active port yeast.
4. Make the quantity up to 3 gallons and ferment on the pulp for 7 days.
5. Strain out the fruit, press lightly, pour the must into a fermentation jar, stir in the rest of the sugar, fit an air lock and continue fermentation in a warm place.
6. When fermentation finishes rack into a clean jar, taste the wine and adjust the sweetness to your palate. Add 1 Camden tablet per gallon and store for 12 months before bottling. Serve free from chill with cheese and apples. The winemaker using an hydrometer should aim to ferment a total specific gravity of 1.120.

Alternative recipes to be made in the same way for 1 gallon are as follows:

1. 4lb ripe blackberries
   2½lb ripe elderberries
   2¾lb sugar
   ¾ oz tartaric acid
   300g grape juice concentrate

2. 4lb ripe morello cherries
   1lb ripe blackberries
   1lb elderberries
   ¾ oz tartaric acid
   250g grape juice concentrate
   2¾lb sugar.
3. 4lb ripe damsons
   1lb ripe blackberries
   1lb ripe elderberries
   ¾ oz tartaric acid
   250g grape juice concentrate
   2¾lb sugar.
4. 2lb blackberries
   2lb blackcurrants
   2lb elderberries
   ¼ oz tartaric acid
   300g grape juice concentrate
   2¾lb sugar.

N.B. Pectic enzyme, Camden tablets and Port yeast and nutrient are required for each recipe.

Some of the ingredients for making 'port'.

7: Some Practical Tips

Crushing Fruit

There are a number of easy ways to solve this problem.

1. Freeze the fruit for 48 hours, thaw it quickly and it will easily crush between fingers.
2. After washing and stalking the fruit, place small quantities at a time in a heavy-grade polythene bag and hit with a steak hammer, rolling pin or mallet. If the bag is too full it may split.
3. Place the fruit in the bottom of a large polythene bin and stamp it with a baulk of hardwood 10″ x 3″ x 3″ attached to a broom handle.
4. Small quantities may be liquidised or put through an electric mixer.
5. A fruit crusher may be bought from firms such as Loftus of Charlotte Street, London W1. This is particularly useful for large quantities of fruit.
6. The juice may be extracted with the aid of the Saftborn steam juice extractor.

Mashing and Fermentation Bins

At the height of the season no one has enough bins in which to mash or ferment. Temporary bins may be made to any size. Select a suitable sized cardboard box, often freely available from grocers and supermarkets. Strengthen it by binding adhesive tape or string around it. Line it with a polythene bag of about 200 gauge—medium heavy—and place a similar bag inside that. (Lighter bags of 120 gauge are not suitable.) Examine both bags carefully before use and test that the seams are waterproof. Alternatively use polythene tubing. Gather one end together in close tucks, tie it tightly then seal it by melting the gathering with a match flame.

New polythene bags are quite sterile and the must may be placed in them without further ado. Gather the top end of the bag together at the surface of the must and place a rubber ring around it. The pressure of the carbon dioxide gas rising from the fermentation will be able to push its way through the neck of the bag and no air will be able to get in. In this way you can adjust the size of your bin to hold whatever quantity is required. There are no air gaps in bins too large for the quantity of must, nor bins so full that they cannot be moved without spilling. This is an inexpensive and efficient way of coping with varying quantities. You can make as little as 1 gallon or as much as ten gallons or more in the same bag.

After use the inner bag may be thrown away and if necessary, the box

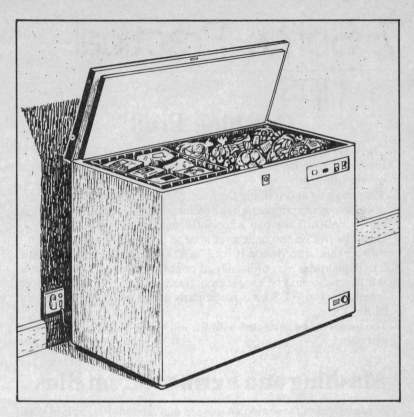

Packs of fruit for winemaking can be kept most satisfactorily in a chest freezer.

collapsed until required again. This is a practical space-saving container, well worth wider adaptation.

It is quite safe to mash and ferment in these bags, but it is not recommended that they be used for storage. Glass or stoneware jars are only surpassed by wooden casks with a minimum capacity of 5 gallons. Smaller casks are unsuitable because their larger ratio of surface to volume causes oxidation of the wine.

Fermentation

Some winemakers have difficulty in finding a suitably warm place for fermentation. There are several solutions, from an electrically heated fermentation pad on which the jar is stood, to an insulated fermentation cupboard warmed with a black-heat electric tube attached to a thermostat. An immersion heater attached to a thermostat is also available for fitting to polythene bins. Cover the bin with blankets by way of insulation.

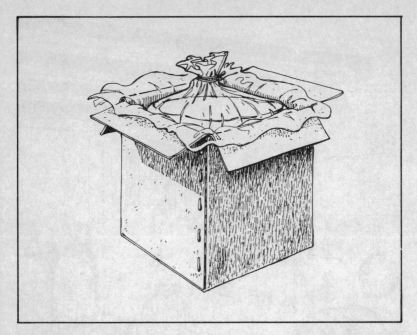

A mashing and fermentation bin made from a cardboard box as suggested on page 40. It is lined with polythene bags, and arranged as described in the text.

Storage

Bottle storage is a problem for many people although it need not be. Cardboard bottle containers are fairly easily obtainable and placed on their side make serviceable bottle racks. The containers may be stacked upon one another to fill many unusually shaped storage places, such as under the stairs, work benches etc.

With the changeover from solid fuel to oil or gas heating in many homes the coal store is no longer needed. Thoroughly cleaned and whitewashed this accomodation makes a very useful cellar for storing wines. It is often brick built and without a window. Provided it has a well fitting door it will insulate the wine from substantial temperature changes during storage.

Cleanliness

Cleanliness of all the equipment used cannot be over-emphasised. It has been said that sulphite is a winemaker's best friend. One tablet dissolved in one gallon of liquid releases 50 p p m of the sterilising gas

sulphur dioxide. 2 tablets dissolved in one pint of tepid water in which half a teaspoonful of citric acid has been dissolved will make a solution that will effectively sterilise everything with which it comes into contact. Rinse each bottle with it, pouring it from bottle to bottle or from jar to jar, soften corks in it, rinse the siphon tube each time it is used, the hydrometer trial jar, the funnel and so on. Drain the items dry and do not rinse them again before use.

After use, wash and sterilise all equipment and put it away clean and dry.

Wash all ingredients before use and unless the ingredients are boiled, sterilise them with a Camden tablet at the rate of 1 per gallon. If the fruit is over-ripe then use 2 tablets.

These simple acts of hygiene will prevent spoilage of your wine by infection from moulds and bacteria.

Keep all jars full to avoid air spaces which cause oxidation and deterioration of the wine. Top the jars up with similar wine or cold boiled water. Sterilised glass marbles may also be used effectively. Only when making and storing sherry-type wine should the jars not be filled and well corked.

Opposite: A coal cellar converted to a winery, with a cask on a stand, an immersion heater and thermostat in a bin, bottles stored in cartons, and convenient stowage for all equipment.

8: Making the most of Your Wine

Maturity

All wine, whether a commercial, everyday wine, an expensive wine for a special occasion or your own 'home brew', deserves proper treatment. Try not to drink it before it is ready for drinking. This may be anything from 3 months to 3 years depending on the individual wine. In general, light and white wines are best drunk young and fresh, while heavier and red wines need longer to mature.

Suitability

When selecting a wine for serving, consider the context in which it will be drunk. Is it to accompany a meal and if so is it to be served with fish, poultry, red meat or the sweet dessert course? On the whole dry white wines taste best with fish, pork and poultry, whilst dry red wines taste best with red meats and cheese. Both these wines are unsuitable for the dessert course, which needs a sweet white wine.

Sparkling wines, dry sherry-type wines and even certain dry white wines, stimulate the appetite before a meal, while strong rich wines are best enjoyed after a meal. Choose a wine suitable for the purpose.

Temperature

Because red wines contain tannin, they need to be served free from chill if they are to be tasted at their best. Conversely white and rosé wines which contain little if any tannin, taste best when they are served cool and crisp. Sparkling wines need to be chilled so that the bubbles do not escape too rapidly when the cork is drawn. A few hours in a warm kitchen is enough to take the chill off a red wine. An hour or so in the refrigerator will crisp a white or rosé wine and sparkling wine which may then be immersed in an ice bucket.

Summer wine cups taste best when chilled with small cubes of ice and slightly sweetened. Winter mulls and punches should be heated only to 140° F. Hotter than this and the alcohol comes off in the vapour. They should never be boiled

Decanters

Few bottles, however attractively decorated, look as well on a table as a clear glass decanter or carafe. Many wine bottles are dark green and some even brown so that the attractive colour and clarity of the wine cannot be seen in the bottle. Furthermore, the pouring of the wine into a carafe or decanter and the short while it remains with a larger surface exposed to the air, enables a young wine to develop a little more bouquet. Fancy labels need not then be stuck on to bottles except those that are to be given away. A very simple label will do for the purpose of identification for selection. Once in the carafe or decanter it can speak for itself!

Glasses

Every wine deserves a decent glass, ie, one with a base, a stem and an incurved bowl. Suitable glasses for various purposes are illustrated. A tulip shaped glass for aperitifs, a goblet for table wine and a tall 'flute' for sparkling wines. This shape shows off best the long beads of sparkling bubbles which are more slowly released than from the saucer-shaped glasses. A much smaller glass is needed for liqueurs of which less is consumed. Only clear glasses should be used, free from colour in bowl, stem or base, free from designs and not too heavily cut or chased. The glass should support the wine unobtrusively.

Company

Few people enjoy drinking wine by themselves. Indeed, people greatly enjoy the fellowship it engenders. When selecting your wine consider also your company. If your guests are confirmed tea or beer drinkers there is little point in offering them your finest dry wine. Offer them tea or beer instead. On the other hand if they have sophisticated palates, select your finest wines knowing that they will be well appreciated. If you are in doubt, pour them just a little wine at first. It is much more pleasing to be asked for more, than to see your guests fiddling with an overful glass of wine that they do not like. In any case never more than half to two-thirds fill a glass. This quantity looks neither greedy nor mean, the glass can be moved without spillage and there is room for the bouquet to collect and be 'nosed' without inconvenience.

Drinking

When serving wine, offer it if possible from a silver salver, so that the reflections enhance the appearance of the wine. Alternatively use any old tray covered with a white cloth. Avoid coloured or patterned trays

Glasses and decanters suitable for the serving of wine. Use goblets for red wine and the longer stemmed goblets for still white wine.

which will vie with the wine for the eye's attention and so detract from the wine.

The glass is best picked up between the fingers and thumb. To hold it by the bowl masks the wine and varies the temperature. It also looks too casual and as though one lacks feeling for the wine.

First hold the bowl towards a good light so that the colour and clarity can be observed and enjoyed. Give the glass a gentle twist so that the wine swirls in the glass, leaving colourless waves of glycerine to return more slowly to the wine. Then pass the bowl beneath your nose, take at first a gentle sniff and then a deeper breath. Enjoy the bouquet and consider how vinous, fruity or flowery it smells. Sometimes you can detect its sweetness or acidity or tannin. There is much to be enjoyed by the discerning nose.

Next take a mouthful of wine, not a tiny sip, move it around your mouth, chew it and swallow it slowly. Open your mouth and take a little breath. It will emphasise the bouquet and flavour. Wait quietly as the various sensations are reported by the different taste buds, especially those on the very back of the palate.

Farewell

These record the wine's 'farewell', the taste, texture and general impression of cleanliness, smoothness, roundness and delight. A

58

good wine will have a long farewell—a taste which lingers on for a minute or more after the wine has been swallowed. When these are all in harmony and perfection, your enjoyment is heightened a hundredfold by knowing that you made it yourself. The effort and waiting suddenly become so very well worthwhile. Alas, this moment of joy is sometimes marred by the realisation that this is the last bottle. Resolve to make much more on the morrow.

9: Further Sources of Information

Publications

The Amateur Winemaker
Published by Amateur Winemaker Publications Ltd, South Street, Andover, Hants.

Home Brewing and Winemaking
Published by Foremost Press Ltd., P.O. Box 1. Wirral, Merseyside.
  Monthly magazines containing a wide variety of articles and advertisements together with news about winemaking clubs and competitions. Obtainable from newsagents or by annual subscription direct from the publishers.

The Boots Book of Winemaking & Brewing.
Illustrated in colour. Only obtainable from Boots the Chemist. Many simple step-by-step recipes.

Making Sparkling Wines, Cyril Lucas. Published by Mills & Boon.

Simple Guide to Home-made Beer, B. C. A. Turner and D. Moon. Published by Mills and Boon.

How to Make Wines with a Sparkle, J. Restall and D. Hebbs. Published by Amateur Winemaker Publications Ltd.

Beer for Beginners, Ken Hill. Published by Mills and Boon.

Home Brew Clubs

More than 1000 clubs exist in towns and villages everywhere. Modest subscriptions to pay for hire of the hall. Opportunities to meet other home winemakers and brewers and to taste their wines and beers. Lectures from experienced members and discussion nights. Affiliation to Regional Federation and National Association. Competitions and Shows. Address from your Civic Centre, Library, GPO, or local newspaper. If these fail ask one of the magazines for details.

Evening Classes

Every Autumn, most Evening Institutes include at least one class for beginners. Ask for details from local Adult Education Office.

Shows

Home Handicraft, Horticultural and Flower Shows often include some basic wine classes in their exhibitions. Look for local advertisements.

Supplies

Equipment and ingredients can be bought from:
(a) The specialist Home Brew shops in almost every town.
(b) The larger branches of Boots the Chemist.
(c) Some other chemists, supermarkets, department stores, garden centres, etc.
(d) Loftus Ltd, Charlotte Street, London W1.
(e) By mail order from the many firms advertising in the magazines mentioned.

BEN TURNER

Ben Turner, author of this book and advisor to the *Home Brew* Thames Television series, started making wine in 1945 and has made wine, mead, beer and liqueurs every year since then. He has written 25 books on this subject including *Boots Book of Winemaking, Pan Book of Winemaking* and *Compleat Winemaker and Brewer at Home*. He has taught evening classes, given lectures and broadcast on wine and beer making. He was co-founder in 1961 of the National Association of Amateur Wine and Beer Makers and was its President in 1971-73. Additionally, he was co-founder in 1962 of the Amateur Winemakers' National Guild of Judges and is still judging wine regularly around the country.

RICHARD BOSTON

Richard Boston, the presenter of *Home Brew*, is well known as a journalist and broadcaster. He has written extensively about wine, beer and pubs, especially in the *Guardian*, to which he contributes a column every Saturday. His books include *An Anatomy of Laughter* and, most recently, *Beer and Skittles*.

WINE PRODUCTION RECORD

Type of Wine

Ingredients

   Quantity of Juice

   S.G.

   Acidity

   Other ingredients

   . . . .

   . . . .

   . . . .

   . . . .

   Water added

   Sugar added

   Type of yeast

Final volume

Final S.G. & Temperature

Acidity

Fermentation started

Fermentation progress

Date					
Temperature					
S.G.					

Dates Racked					

Date Bottled

Tasting   Date   Remarks

WINE PRODUCTION RECORD

Type of Wine

Ingredients

    Quantity of Juice

    S.G.

    Acidity

    Other ingredients

    . . . .

    . . . .

    . . . .

    . . . .

    Water added

    Sugar added

    Type of yeast

Final volume

Final S.G. & Temperature

Acidity

Fermentation started

Fermentation progress

Date					
Temperature					
S.G.					

Dates Racked					

Date Bottled

Tasting   Date   Remarks